BUDDHISM

Mani stones (large painted stones found along
village routes), inscribed with 'Om Mane Padme
Hum' (literally, 'Hail the Jewel in the Lotus', the
jewel being a symbol of the Buddha),
symbolise self-realisation and are a
prominent feature of Tibetan Buddhism.

ISBN: 1-85605-556-6

Published in 2000 by **Silverdale Books**
An imprint of **Bookmart Ltd**
Registered Number 2372865
Trading as Bookmart Limited
Desford Road, Enderby
Leicester, LE9 5AD

© **Lustre Press Pvt. Ltd., 1997**
M-75, Greater Kailash-II Market
New Delhi-110 048, INDIA

Photographs:
Jean Lois NOU, Aditya Arya, B.P.S. Walia
Devendra Basnet, Joanna Van Gruisen, Kabir
Khan, Mani Lama, Pramod Kapoor

Printed and bound at Singapore

BUDDHISM

Pushpesh Pant

Silverdale Books

Contents

The Buddha
of the Past

Extract the sesame oil of your
body,
Clarify this liquid as conceptual
thought,
And pour the purified oil
Into the vessel of mind's empty
nature.

Then, ignite the wick
Spun from the twin cords of
appearance and emptiness
With the flame of knowledge and
pure awareness.

Thus shall the gloom of ignorance
be dispelled,
And you shall abide for time
beyond time
In the inexhaustible, incomparable
pleasure of liberation.

Queen Maya's dream foretelling
Buddha's celestial birth has
provided the inspiration for this
painting from Ajanta (India).

Legend tells us that some two thousand and five hundred years ago, there lived a noble chieftain named Shuddhodhan belonging to the martial clan of the Sakya, who had his capital at Kapilvastu, on what today comprises the Indo-Nepal border in the Himalayan foothills. One day, as Shuddhodhan's wife, Mahamaya, lay resting in the palace grounds she had an unusual dream. She experienced the vision of a majestic white elephant entering her womb. This was interpreted by the royal astrologers as an auspicious tiding indicating that she would soon deliver an extraordinary child. Tradition also maintains that when the child was born he indeed displayed thirty-two *lakshana* or signs designating a *mahapurush*—great man— and a *chakravartin*—universal victor. However, destiny had planned other things for the child. He did not grow up to become a great conqueror, invincible in the feat of arms. He became the *buddh* or Buddha—the enlightened one who has supreme knowledge—and won the souls of millions through his words and wisdom.

Historians do not agree on many of Buddha's biographical details, as they are reluctant to uncritically accept as 'fact' something that has obviously been embellished with fancy by the faithful over generations. Yet, though dates and details may be disputed, the substance of the story remains intact. There *was* a person of noble birth born in that period who renounced a life of comfort and pleasure to pursue spiritual knowledge. After years of austerities and philosophical quest he finally attained knowledge that liberated him from the shackles that hold mortals in bondage to misery. He became an itinerant monk and preached sermons for almost five decades. By the time he died he had become a legend and his teachings enjoyed a cult following. The path he showed was taken by many, and soon identified as a new religion.

The child ushered into the world by a strangely symbolic dream was named Siddharth—one who has accomplished his aim in life. He was also known as Gautam as he was born in the clan of Gautam. His mother died soon after his birth and he was nursed and brought up by his aunt.

The legends of the Buddha's life are preserved in the *Jataka* tales which are a collection of five hundred and fifty stories of the former lives of the Buddha. The *Jataka* tales recount incidents from many past births of the Buddha. They include picaresque romances, dramatic parables and fairy tales. These provide insightful glimpses into the life and teachings of the Buddha and have inspired great works of art in India and in foreign lands.

The *Jataka* tales say that young Siddharth, steeped in luxury, was unaware of things like old age or sickness or death. His father, warned by a soothsayer, took exceptional care to shelter the boy from whatever was unpleasant. One day, while enjoying a pleasant ride in his chariot, Siddharth saw an toothless old man bent with age, toothless, with hair all gray, hobbling painfully with the aid of a stick. He asked the chariot driver about this strange person and was told that this was nothing unusual—old age and such disability were the lot of all men. On another occasion Siddharth witnessed the suffering of a seriously ill man in distress and found out that this too was not uncommon. Not long afterwards, he came across a cortege and learnt that this is what must come to pass for all those that live. He came face to face with the harsh reality that the sheltered life in the palace had shielded him from. Deeply sensitive and intelligent, he could not escape the conclusion that man on earth was subject to inevitable suffering. He could not help asking, 'How can the pain be avoided, misery reduced?' And, when he saw a yellow robed recluse he began to think, 'Isn't this the best way to live—away from pleasure and pain?'

When he received the news that a son had been born to him, it brought him no happiness—only his agitation increased. 'Man is only born to suffer disease and decay in this life', he reflected. 'What if I were to go in search of a truth that frees from this pain?' The turmoil in his mind continued for many days.

Ashvagosh, a Buddhist writer and poet of the first century AD, has, in his poem *Buddhacharitam*, painted a vivid, if revolting, picture of an incident that, it is believed, proved to be a turning point in Siddharth's life. The young prince was usually entertained by beautiful women skilled in music and dance. These revels brought him no joy. He listlessly participated in such soirée without any enthusiasm. One day, he fell asleep during the performance. The lovely lasses too, laid down their instruments and tried to snatch some rest. When Siddharth woke up he was greeted by the ugly sight of the drowsy maidens lying dishevelled after the night of revelry. Ashvagosh writes: 'One lay with her skirt fallen from her loins like a woman crushed by an elephant; another breathed violently and yawned with her mouth agape—arms distorted, with ornaments and garlands in disarray. They lay sprawled as if intoxicated, without any beauty, as if dead. One had saliva drivelling from her mouth, another ground her teeth. The room was like a lake strewn with broken lotus stems—a charnel full of corpses.'

The scene filled Siddharth with great disgust. After witnessing the transformation of delightful maidens into such unattractive creatures he became even more disenchanted with sensual pleasures. He found this existence insufferable. He had been contemplating a spiritual life for long and this was the last straw. He decided to renounce his comfortable life.

Siddharth Gautam's renunciation, we must understand, was not an escape from the world of pain and struggle—it was a turning away from daydreams and indulgence in idle pleasures. Gautam, we are told, left his home one dark night when he was almost thirty. He was no callow romantic youth then but a mature householder with a wife and a son. The dramatic departure was not the impulsive reaction of a melancholic and hypersensitive youth suffering from *ennui*, nor was it

Following pages 10-11: A procession of Buddhist monks at the famous Hemis monastery in Ladakh (India).

the result of a connected series of incidents that led to a climax. The great departure (*mahabhinishkramana*) was a serious and grave decision, not one undertaken in haste. In retrospect, this was not an escape from the strife and suffering of the material world but a serious effort to cope with it.

On the night when he decided to depart from his home, he woke up Channa, the charioteer, and commanded him to saddle his horse, Kantaka. As the horse was being readied Siddharth was overcome by an urge to have a last look at his wife and child. He went back to the bed-chamber and gazed in the flickering light of the oil lamp at his wife, Yashodhara, and son, Rahul, asleep on a soft bed strewn with jasmine flowers. The temptation was strong to hold the child in his arms for one last time but he resisted it fearing that this may wake up his wife and weaken his resolve to leave home.

Siddharth went first into the city of Kapilvastu, renowned for its learned teachers. He approached Allar Kalama, a famed ascetic, to seek spiritual guidance. But his mind found no peace here. He learnt about Yoga, the routine of a holy life, and meditation from many sages but these learned persons could not satisfy his curiosity about the final release from sorrow. Having served a period of discipleship diligently, he moved on to other teachers and reputed places of pilgrimage in search of mental peace.

Many months were spent in restless wandering before he settled down under a pipal (*Ficus religiosa*) tree by a river, with the resolve that he would not get up until he had attained supreme knowledge. He practised severe austerities and exposed his body to unbearable rigours. The physical discomforts were acute but the mental agony was no less disturbing. The young ascetic denied himself food, shelter and protective clothing. He starved his body and allowed his good looks to waste away. As he told his disciples many years later, 'My body reached a state of utter exhaustion. Just like a knot of grass or rush became my bone-joints through poor nourishment. Just like a bison's hoof became my hinder parts. Just like a row of reed knots my backbone stood out. Just as the rafters of the tottering house fall in, this way and that way, so did my ribs. Just as in very deep well sparkles water down below so did the lustre of my eyes in deep sockets.'

Recollecting his struggles during the years of wandering, the Buddha once told Sariputta, one of his earliest and most steadfast disciples, of the harsh penance and persistent self-doubt. 'I was doing penance outdoing other ascetics. As I stayed alone in the forest perhaps a deer

Facing page: This exquisitely adorned figure from Ajanta is Avalokitesvara, probably the most popular *bodhisattva* (the compassionate one) in Buddhism. **Following pages 14-15:** The three daughters of Mara, the evil tempter, portrayed here represent the illusion of desire, tenderness and delight—all apparently attractive and experts in the art of seduction. The Buddha was able to pierce the illusion and found them repulsive and pitiable.

would come to me, or a peacock—sometimes a twig would fall, maybe a breeze rustled through the fallen leaves. I was startled . . . then I began to think, why do I have this constant fear? I did not stand still nor did I sit or lie down. I spent the night walking up and down until I had bent to my will that panic and terror.'

Later biographers of the Buddha have invested these incidents with symbolic significance. The Buddha is shown grappling with demons and evil spirits during this period. Mara, the evil tempter, we are told, assaulted the meditating Siddharth and tried to lure him away. The graphic description by the poet, Ashvagosh in *Buddhacharitam,* captures the drama of this conflict powerfully,

> The ocean rose under the vibrations of a whirlwind.
> The ocean rose under the vibrations of this earthquake;
> rivers flowed back towards the sources;
> peaks of lofty mountains where countless trees
> had grown for ages rolled crumbling to the earth;
> a fierce storm howled all around . . . the very sun
> enveloped itself in darkness, and a host of
> headless spirits loomed in the sky.

Siddharth realised that it is difficult to reach noble knowledge surpassing mortality with a body so exhausted. He decided to take some nourishment to sustain the body so that the spiritual pursuit could continue. One day Sujata, a peasant girl, mistaking him for a tree-dwelling spirit, brought him an offering of rice cooked in milk and the enfeebled ascetic ate it, to recover his strength, and resumed his meditations.

On the forty-ninth day after he had taken his seat under a pipal tree on the banks of the river Niranjana near modern Gaya, he saw light. As H.G. Wells has remarked in *A Short History of the World*, 'When the mind grapples with a great and intricate problem, it makes advances, it secures its positions step by step, with but little realization of the gains it has made, until suddenly with an effect of abrupt illumination it realises its victory. So it would appear to have happened to Gautama.'

Siddharth had now become the Buddha—the Enlightened One and the Tathagata. As the *Samyutta Nikaya,* the third book of a part of the canon containing Buddha's discourses, tells us, 'The Tathagata is one who doth cause a way to arise which had not arisen before; who is the knower of a way, who understands a way and who is skilled in a way.' Although often referred to as Tathagata—'one who has come and gone thus', Gautam (or Siddharth) is best known as the Buddha.

After initial hesitation, the Buddha decided to venture out into the world and teach others what he had realised. At first he felt, 'Men cling to what they cling. If I were to teach them the truth, others would not understand, and that would be a waste of my effort which would hurt me.' But then he weighed this against another thought, 'Not every man or woman is unwilling to see the truth, but they need to be told about it.' His compassion for mankind finally overcame all doubts.

The first to hear the Buddha's discourse were the five Brahmins who had once been his companions in penance. They had parted company with him greatly disappointed when he decided to sustain himself by taking nourishment that he had earlier forsaken. It was to them that the Buddha preached his first sermon at *mrigdav*—the deer park—at Sarnath near Benares. It is believed that the first time the Buddha spoke of Nirvana (final liberation from the bonds of existence) and the right path was on a full moon night in July at this deer park. This event is referred to as the *Dharmchakrapravartan*—setting in motion the Wheel of Law. Aptly, the subject of the first sermon was to explain the value of the middle way. The Brahmins had left him as he had abandoned extreme austerities. Now the Buddha told them that self-torture was as unworthy as a life of luxury for the seeker of the noble truth. Extremes must be avoided as both pleasure and pain distract the mind from its purpose. The Buddha used a familiar analogy—that of the string of the *vina*, a musical instrument that cannot produce melody if it is slack, but which breaks if made too taut.

The Buddha's teachings struck a sympathetic chord in the hearts of his contemporaries. By this time the sublime speculations of the Upanishads (the later Hindu scriptures), had yielded pride of place to expensive ritual. The caste system had become rigid and oppressive. Society was in ferment and the polity in flux. Economic enterprise was flourishing. The intellectual climate was right for mounting a challenge to orthodoxy. What also helped was the conversion of powerful princes and rich traders to the Buddhist way of life. Royal patronage and generous endowments allowed the Buddha's teachings to travel far and wide. King Ashok (272-232 BC) of the Mauryan dynasty, the first Indian king recognized as 'emperor', converted to Buddhism after his heart was filled with remorse upon seeing bloodshed during a war. He sent his son and daughter—Mahendra and Sanghmitara—on a religious mission to Sri Lanka. He also erected massive stone pillars and got them inscribed with edicts to instruct his people about *dhamma* or the way shown by the Buddha. These royal edicts were distributed throughout the vast extent of the Mauryan Empire.

Buddhism continued to flourish in India and beyond its borders. The five centuries after Buddha's delivering his first sermon at Sarnath were a period of exciting expansion within the subcontinent and in foreign lands. Taxila near the north-western frontier emerged as a centre of Buddhist learning and Gandhara, the name given to north-western India (before the partition of the country) by Alexander the Great, became famous as the seat of a vibrant and influential art style specializing in Buddhist iconography. Buddhism travelled smoothly via the silk route through Central Asia to Turkestan and thence to China and Mongolia.

In eastern India, Nalanda and Vikramshila, which used to be in Bihar, rivalled Taxila. Buddhist influence radiated from these glorious *vihars* (Buddhist monastic establishments) in all directions. The Buddhist missionaries found the spice route conducive. Traders embarking from the ports of Tamralipti (Tamluk) and Bhrigukaccha (Broach) for

Yavadvipa (Java), Suvarnadvipa (Sumatra), Champa (Cambodia and Vietnam) carried with their other precious cargo the priceless gems of Buddhism. Kanishka (AD 80), the Kushana emperor, too was an enthusiastic adherent to the new faith and provided powerful patronage. It was during his reign that a great council of Buddhists was convened. Foreigners continued to evince a lively interest in Buddhist doctrine. King Milind's (the Greek king Menander) inquiries were profound enough to be collected in a separate book, *Milindpanho,* in 100 BC, that soon acquired an almost canonical status. In the seventh century, King Harsha, who had earlier been a devout follower of Lord Shiva (one of the gods of the Hindu trinity), also converted to Buddhism.

The first two centuries following the birth of Christ saw the construction of the grand *stupa* (mound-like structures which are built over the relics of the Buddha and other Buddhist saints) at Sanchi, and the *chaitya-vihar* (prayer-halls) at Bharhut and Amaravati. Buddhism had obviously become a popular and diffuse religion as it is difficult to imagine that persecuted followers of an unpopular, minority cult could have undertaken such ambitious and expensive activities.

The accounts of foreign travellers testify to flourishing Buddhist monasteries. Buddhism continued to receive state support in the time of the Pala rulers of Bengal in the 10th-11th centuries. If Buddhism declined successively in the land of its birth it was not due to want of patronage. The causes have to be searched elsewhere. One explanation is the reform of Hinduism and emergence of Bhakti, the devotional form of Hinduism. The Buddha himself was incorporated as one of the ten Hindu *avtars*—incarnations of the supreme being —and Buddhism in its popular version became, in fact, indistinguishable from many Brahmanical cults. A more important factor was the revival of Hinduism and its reform. Sankara, a famous Hindu philosopher, travelled across the land debating with Buddhist monks and polemically getting the better of them. For the common man, Buddhism became another cult.

In any case, if we wish to encounter Buddhism meaningfully, a mere review of historical facts is not going to be of much help. To understand why the existential dilemma faced by a young man—who was born centuries before the birth of Christ—continues to move us today and retains relevance, we must leave the domain of history and move over to the realm of myth, legend, folklore, and of course, stimulating metaphysics.

The four noble truths

What the Buddha preached at Sarnath were the *Chatvari Arya Satyani*—the Four Noble Truths—and the *Aryashtanga Marg*—the Noble

Facing page: Secluded monasteries like Rumtek (Sikkim) are ideal for contemplating the Four Noble Truths preached by the Buddha, which say that the root cause of human suffering is desire and all desire has to be stemmed to achieve liberation.

Eightfold Path. He asked rhetorically, 'There are two ends not to be served by the wanderer. What are these two? The pursuit of desire and of pleasure which springs from desire, which is base, common, leading to rebirth, ignoble and unprofitable; and the pursuit of pain and hardship which is grievous, ignoble and unprofitable. The middle way of the Tathagata avoids both these ends . . .'

He also spoke of ultimate nature of existence which is sorrow, 'And, this is the noble truth of sorrow. Birth is sorrow, age is sorrow, disease is sorrow, death is sorrow, contact with the unpleasant is sorrow, separation from the pleasant is sorrow, every unfulfilled wish is sorrow—in short all five components of individuality are sorrow.'

The four noble truths that the Buddha propagated are: *dukh* (misery), *dukh samudaya* (advent of misery), *nirodh* (restraint of misery) and *marg* (the way that liberates us from misery). *Dukh* is the human condition—eternal misery. Age, that renders us infirm, is misery. Separation from the beloved is misery. Union with unpleasant persons and circumstances is misery. Illness is misery, and the fear of death is misery. No one can hope to liberate himself from this miserable existence unless the root cause of misery is identified.

The world we live in becomes painful, Buddha said, because we approach it through the mediacy of desire (*trishna*). This desire yearns for eternity and everything is transient. The Buddha taught that there are other ways of experiencing reality than desire. Desire, again, is another condition, not a thing in itself. By oneself one suffers and by oneself one ceases to suffer.

A serene Buddha and his retinue of followers: a panel representative of the Amravati school. A striking example of Buddhist iconography.

Buddha pointed out that what causes anguish is desire. *Trishna*—literally translated as insatiable thirst—is the craving for sensual pleasure that leads ultimately to painful webs of attachment. Abjuring desire is imperative for *nirvana* which is a complete cessation of being and the supreme goal of Buddhist endeavour.

To attain this goal, Buddha prescribed the Eight-fold Path, also referred to as *Majjhima Patipada*—the middle way. The description is quite apt as the Buddha eschewed alike harsh austerities and the soft life.

The Eight-fold Path laid great emphasis on right conduct, right views, right intentions, right action, right livelihood, right effort, right mindfulness, right recollection and right contemplation. It needs to be remembered that 'right' in the discourses of Buddha did not have an absolutist connotation but a relativistic one. The supreme test of righteousness was compassion—*karuna*.

In consonance with the Buddha's first sermons also took place the founding of the holy order—the Buddhist Sangha. Rules were laid down for admission to the order after administering the oath:

Buddham sharanam gacchami,
dhammam sharanam gacchami,
sangham sharanam gacchami

(I take my refuge in the Buddha/the true path/and the order).

These subsequently are referred to as *triratna*—the three gems. There were detailed rules for the Sangha followers for regular assembly, collecting alms, retreat to approved places of residence during the rainy season and for everyday life. In general, there were restrictions on idle gossip, evil friends and pleasure-seeking. The monks were advised to be self-possessed and composed.

Initially there had been no prescribed code of conduct for a Buddhist monk. He was expected to be non-violent, celibate, austere and conscientious. He was seen as a free member of a free community. With the passage of time, the need was felt to impose some discipline to keep the members of the Sangha united and a generally accepted set of practices became the custom. The daily life of a Buddhist monk is chiefly spent in the study of scriptures and religious rites. He is expected to share in the work of the monastery which involves cleaning his cell and sweeping the courtyard. Among the most important exercises is *brahmavihar*—meditating while sitting cross-legged. The monk seeks to fill his mind with four sublime moods—or virtues—of Buddhism: love,

Facing page: The tranquillity of Dhammeka Stupa at Sarnath continues to draw pilgrims and monks.
Following pages 24-25: This contemporary painting depicts *karuna* or compassion which comprises the core of Buddhism. The Buddha practised what he preached throughout his life. He accorded priority to relieving suffering and recognised no social barriers. Herein lay the great appeal of the new creed.

pity, joy and serenity. The monks are administered ten vows when they are ordained. These include, among other things, celibacy, abstinence from intoxicants, no solid food after midday. The monk has to beg for his food every day and allowed only three accessories, a razor, a needle, an alms bowl. There is no central authority to control or govern the monastic order. The monks assemble every fortnight in *upvasatha*, an act of general confession. A long list of monastic rules from the canonical text of *Vinaya Pitaka* is read out and monks confess one by one to their individual transgressions. If the breach is serious, a monk could be expelled. The ceremony concludes with the preaching of a sermon.

Years as an itinerant monk

The Buddha spent the next forty-five years of his life roaming the land to spread his gospel. The Buddha, it appears, returned to Kapilvastu after enlightenment and converted some members of his family. Devdatta—a villainous rival from the days of adolescence and also his brother-in-law—joined for a while his band of disciples. But as the *Jataka* tales document, Devdatta was a constant source of disgruntled dissent and spread disaffection. Finally he revolted and founded his own short-lived religious order. But many members of the Buddha's family did join the latter. Anand, a cousin, was his favourite and a constant companion in the last phase of his life. Buddha's wife, Yashodhara, sent Rahul to him to claim his patrimony and the young lad was initiated as an acolyte monk.

Angulimal, a dreaded brigand who was notorious for killing his victims and wearing a necklace fashioned from the unfortunate wayfarer's fingers, was won over in the twentieth year of his ministry. Ambapali, a beautiful courtesan, gave up her life of pleasure and followed in the footsteps of the Buddha without flinching.

The dialogues of the Buddha preserved in canonical works introduce us to Sariputta and Maugglayan—both Brahmins—who were with their beloved teacher all the time. The Buddha did not attach any significance to caste or class. Upali, a barber, was equally dear to him as was the millionaire trader Sudatta, nicknamed Aanathpindak which means one who feeds orphans. It was he who bought from a prince the Jetvana, a shaded grove that became the favourite retreat of the Buddha in course of time and the venue of many of his important discourses.

The Buddha visited Kosala, with its capital at Sravasti, several times where reigned King Pasenadi (Prasenjit) who was acknowledged as their suzerain by the Sakyas. Prasenjit was an admirer of the Buddha and honoured him. The Buddha occasionally visited Vatsa with Kosambi

Facing page: The Buddha's gentle and persuasive ways wrought many 'miracles', like the change of heart brought about in the blood-thirsty bandit, Angulimal, who derived his name from the garland he wore, made of the fingers of his victims.

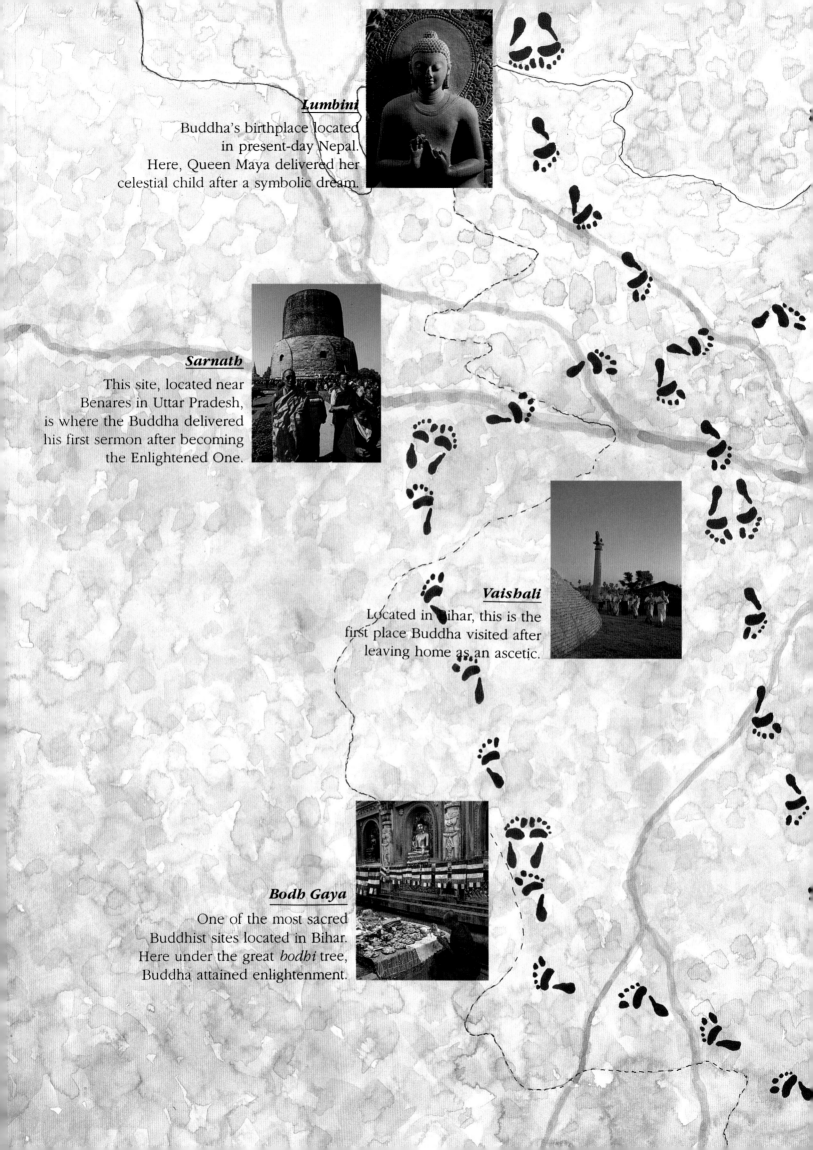

Lumbini

Buddha's birthplace located
in present-day Nepal.
Here, Queen Maya delivered her
celestial child after a symbolic dream.

Sarnath

This site, located near
Benares in Uttar Pradesh,
is where the Buddha delivered
his first sermon after becoming
the Enlightened One.

Vaishali

Located in Bihar, this is the
first place Buddha visited after
leaving home as an ascetic.

Bodh Gaya

One of the most sacred
Buddhist sites located in Bihar.
Here under the great *bodhi* tree,
Buddha attained enlightenment.

ON BUDDHA'S TRAIL
From Birth to Nirvana

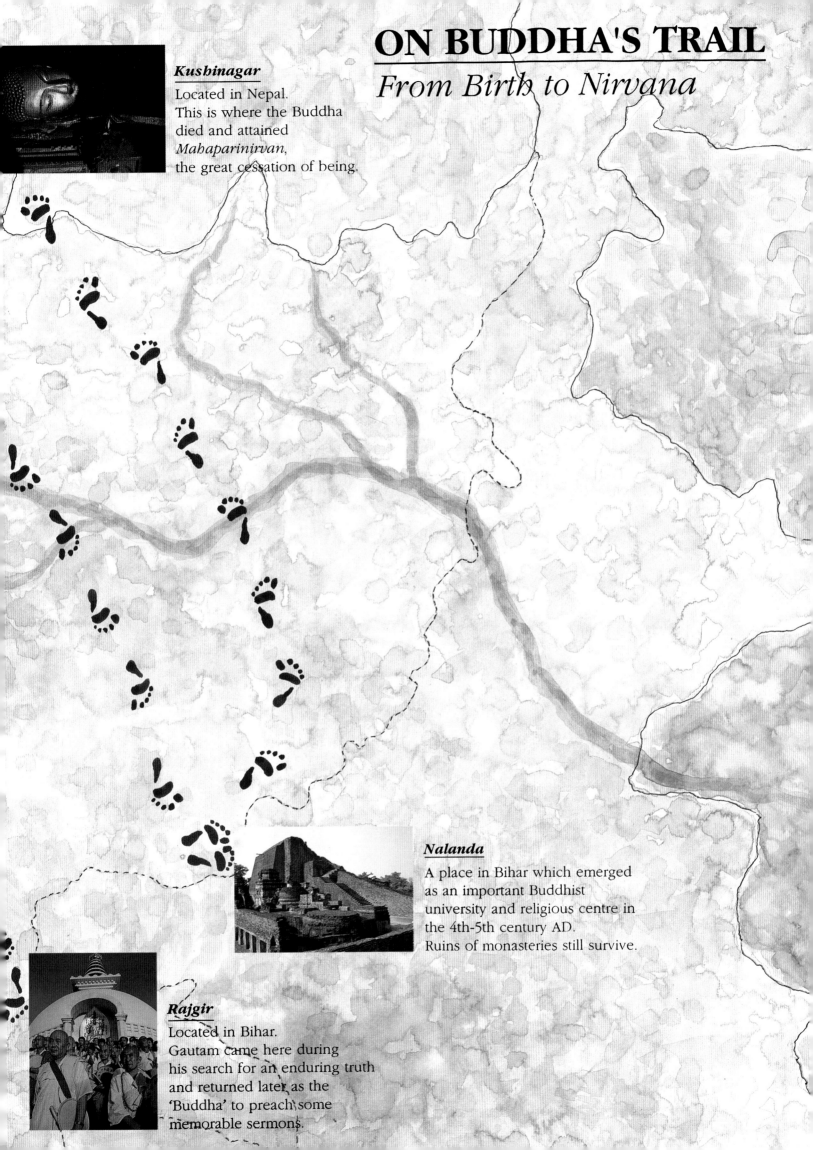

Kushinagar

Located in Nepal.
This is where the Buddha
died and attained
Mahaparinirvan,
the great cessation of being.

Nalanda

A place in Bihar which emerged
as an important Buddhist
university and religious centre in
the 4th-5th century AD.
Ruins of monasteries still survive.

Rajgir

Located in Bihar.
Gautam came here during
his search for an enduring truth
and returned later as the
'Buddha' to preach some
memorable sermons.

as its capital. He often travelled to Rajgir and Gaya, south of the river Ganga. The ruler of Magadh, Bimbisara, was also favorably inclined to Buddhist ideas. To the east, he went as far as Vaishali in the Licchavi domain and Kushinagar in Malla territory. To get some idea of the distances covered, it is useful to remember that approximately 350 kilometres separate Kapilvastu from Gaya, and Kosambi and Vaishali are about 400 kilometres apart. The arduousness of the Buddha's missionary journeys can be imagined in those days when no comfortable or speedy mode of travel existed.

The last person to be converted personally by the Buddha was Subhadda, who received instruction from the master as he reclined on his death bed. This was the time when eastern and northern India were divided into sixteen states or *janpadas*. To the west of the territory of the Sakyas—the Buddha's own people—lay Kosala, the region where Ayodhya and Benares exist today; to the south, the kingdom of Magadh, roughly corresponding to present day south Bihar; to the east resided the Licchavis and Mallas in the region that today forms northern Bihar. Beyond Kosala stretched Vatsa (Allahabad region) and the land of Kurus around Delhi and Mathura.

During his wandering ministry, the Buddha delivered many powerful sermons. He was not a worker of miracles but moved men with words. The evocative spell of these sermons has survived the passage of hundreds of years. Once when a young mother came to him with the body of her dead child with a request that he should restore the child back to life, the Buddha did not refuse outright. He told her to go in search of some mustard seeds brought from a house that had not experienced any bereavement. The lady lost no time in embarking on the prescribed errand. She returned to the Buddha after some time having realised the futility of her search and recognizing that she was not alone in her loss. Not only did she receive a lesson in compassion but also was consoled realistically.

One of the most moving sermons delivered by the Buddha is the fire sermon delivered during his stay at the Elephant Rock near Gaya in the vicinity of the verdant valley of Rajgir. As the Buddha sat surrounded by his disciples in this temporary retreat, a fire broke out one evening in the forest on the opposite hill. The clouds in the sky reflected the crimson hue of the wild flames leaping skyward, streaking like lightning through the billowing smoke. The congregation was spellbound by the fierce blaze.

For the Buddha, the blaze in the forest became a metaphor. 'Everything, O monks,' said he, 'is in flames. The eye is in flames. The visible is in flames. The knowledge of the visible is in flames. Everything is consumed by subtle and invisible flames. Be it pleasure,

Facing page: The miracle at Sravasti where, according to legend, the Buddha dazzled his disbelievers by providing them with a vision of countless Buddhas preaching the noble truth: Ajanta.

Buddhism in its pristine form did not have any place for idols. The *stupa* which housed a holy relic was considered sacred. With time, the *stupa* became a shrine where a formal, respectful *parikrama*—circumambulatory walk—was performed.

be it pain, or be it neither pleasure nor pain, this also is in flames. By what is this fire kindled? By the fire of desire, by the fire of hate, by the fire of fascination. By birth, by old age and death it is kindled . . . this I say, O monks.'

There is a beautiful passage in another sermon where the Buddha names five major rivers and says, 'Just as their waters lose their names and separateness when they flow out to the mighty ocean, so are the castes and ranks and the lineage forgotten when the followers of the Buddha join his order as monks.'

Once the Buddha was asked by Maugglayan, the Brahman follower, 'Are all followers of Buddha sure to get liberation from the world's sorrows?' The Buddha responded with a counter-question, 'Do you know the road to Rajgriha?' When Maugglayan answered in the affirmative, the Buddha said, 'Can you direct a wayfarer on this road?' Maugglayan again answered in the affirmative. Then the Buddha said, 'One wayfarer may reach Rajgriha as directed by you but another may fail to reach. I too just show the way. Some of my followers make it, some do not.'

Facing page: Bodhgaya. Ritual offerings made during Buddhist worship are almost the same as in Hinduism. Flowers, foodgrains, incense and fragrant water are used which create a symphony of colours.

As he grew older, the Tathagata headed towards places he had known as a child and in his youth. His last journey was undertaken when he was almost eighty years of age and in frail health. He was travelling to Kushinara accompanied by Anand when he accepted the hospitality of Kunda, a blacksmith in Pava. Poor Kunda served him a meal comprising boar's flesh and rice.

Perhaps the diet was too rich for the old and ailing master or maybe it had got spoilt. Soon after consuming it the Buddha fell ill. He was in sharp pain and stricken by a severely upset stomach. But he continued on his journey eastward. On the way he soon became dehydrated and collapsed, exhausted, under a tree. Anand was sent to fetch some water from a river nearby. Revived after a brief rest, he insisted on continuing.

As usual, the monks set up their camp in a grove outside the city. Here, the Buddha called his disciples and told them that the end was near and they were not to blame or admonish Kunda for serving the meal. Anand broke down and began to sob.

The Buddha consoled him with what was in fact his last stirring sermon, 'Enough Anand! Do not let yourself be troubled. Do not weep. It is in the very nature of things, that we separate ourselves from them, leave what is most dear to us. Anything born carries within it the seeds of dissolution. Why then the suffering? Be earnest in your efforts to be free from the cancer of sensuality, individuality and ignorance. Brethren, I impress upon you that decay is inherent in all things! Work for your own salvation—be lamps unto yourself!'

This statue from Kushinara (Nepal) shows the *Mahaparinirvana,* the great decease of the Buddha. The Master is shown at though in a state of serene repose.

35

Philosophy and Teachings

This great horn, built cell by cell
From appearances and fixed notions,
Is destroying your happiness,
For attachment to seemingly concrete
objects
Is always a cause for suffering.

But these objects of desire
Have no real existence.
Events have no more reality
Than clouds swirling through the sky.
How then can birth, life, or death
Harm or profit us in any way?

When both the knower and
that which is known
Are essentially emptiness,
How can the pure nature of mind
Be affected in any way at all.

The teachings of the Buddha, believed to have been transmitted in his own words, are found lovingly copied in manuscript scrolls, sanctified, and preserved in miniature caskets in libraries regarded as repositories of sacred objects. Thikse Monastery, Ladakh.

Gautam, after he had really become Siddharth—that is, achieved his aim in life—and been enlightened with knowledge, spoke from the heart and to the common man. To reach the masses he used the folk idiom Pali. It was only many years later that Buddhist philosophers began to debate the subtler points of his metaphysics in Sanskrit—the language of the learned people.

In one of the last sermons delivered by him the Buddha had said, 'Herein, O monks, let a brother, as he dwells in the body, so regard the body that he, being strenuous, thoughtful, and mindful, may, whilst in the world, overcome the grief arising from the craving which follows our sensations—and so also when he thinks or reasons, or feels, let him overcome the grief which arises from the craving due to ideas, or reasoning or feeling.' Out of this simple sermon was later developed the impressive and at times confusing concept of dependent origination— *paticca samuppada*. According to this metaphysics, out of Ignorance arises Imagination, thence Self-consciousness, from it Name and Form, then follow the Six Senses. From these arise Contact and Feeling. These engender Craving and Attachment. This in turn leads to Becoming and Rebirth, and all the ills flesh is heir to.

The way itself is the goal

This metaphysics eventually underlay the need and virtue of following the middle path. Of the eight noble elements of the path, two relate to an outlook on life, three comprise ethical principles, followed by three kinds of mental disciplines. The right view demands an awareness of the suffering a man is subject to in life, the right aim can only be the extinction of this suffering. This means giving up craving. Together, the two would help develop an outlook that prepares a person for liberation of the self. Right speech means abstaining from lying, from abuse, idle gossip. Right action prohibits taking life, or indulging in impulsive acts crazed by lust or anger. Right living forbids earning a livelihood by wrong-doing. Right effort, the Buddha said, meant applying one's mind to defeat evil, right mindedness is to be alert and in control of one's feelings, perceptions and actions. Right recollection and right meditation assist the constant striving to cultivate greater and greater detachment.

Following the middle path reduces morality to a function of human intelligence—a kind of honest self-criticism. The teachings of the Buddha are neither a measuring rod, nor dogma nor a code but the focus—a point of integration for the psyche. There is, however, insistence on discipline.

The Buddha's interpretation of life on earth is essentially a psychological one. Tragic affirmation of pain is his starting point. The psychological critique falls outside the grasp of mere logic. Only the ignorant would charge Gautam of morbidity. Pain itself is a condition, not

Facing page: The first sermon preached by the Buddha at Sarnath is often referred to as the *Dharmachakrapravartan*—Turning the Wheel of Law, represented by the gesture of the hands. Sarnath Museum.

a finality. A universal condition, nonetheless a condition. One may disagree with this diagnosis but what cannot be denied is that the explanation he offered is remarkable for its lucidity and comprehensiveness. The great Buddhist text, *Dhammapada,* says 'By oneself one suffers.' And not because of some fall from grace or due to divine wrath.

Teachings

The kernel of the Buddha's teachings consists of a moral code for living, free of tensions and at peace, with oneself and nature. It is crucial to understand that the Buddhist metaphysical concepts are not just another variant of the doctrine of illusion *(maya).* It would be more correct to interpret these as a doctrine of relativity. All our knowledge is of relations, of conditions—not absolutes or finalities.

'Verily, I declare unto you,' said the Buddha, 'that this very body, mortal as it is, and only a fathom high, but conscious and endowed with mind is the world, and waxing and waning thereof and the way that leads to the passing away thereof.' Gautam laid great emphasis on being straightforward and intelligible. His terms are always crystal clear, never ambiguous. The Buddha categorically denied the existence of God and the permanent nature of the soul. He made man the measure of his world.

What then is reality? The Buddha realised that no matter how deep we probe there exist further levels of analyses. Whichever direction we may choose to move in, there arise ever widening or ever narrowing circles.

In Buddha's time, a bewildering diversity of views prevailed about the existence of God. People debated a whole gamut of probabilities—from polytheism to atheism. Gautam's own position was that of an agnostic. It seems that he was quite content to take the universe for granted and to understand its internal laws and relations. It may not have been a heroic stance but had the virtue of being compatible with common sense. 'Whether my teaching reveals the beginning of things or not, it leads to the thorough destruction of the ill for the doer thereof.'

The Buddha was sceptical of a God in the sense of a personal creator, presiding over the universe. He did not spend energy in defining the term theologically or mystically. He once asked a Brahmin 'Is there a single one of the Brahmans well versed in the three Vedas who has seen the Brahma [the all-pervading] face to face?' He told his followers that all claims to be 'Brahmans' (Brahmins), versed though they be in the three Vedas, is foolish talk. He compared such persons to a man who builds a staircase to reach up into a mansion which neither he nor any one else has seen.

The Buddha did not believe that it was necessary to retain the concept of God for moral-utilitarian purposes. He regarded the universe in manifestation as self-sufficient, that could and did function without divine intervention. This position was already implicit in the dualist philosophy

Previous page 40: A lama punctuating his prayers with drum beats at the Phyang monastery in Ladakh. **Page 41:** A monk deeply engrossed in the study of scriptures in the library of a monastery in Sikkim.

The scene here recreates the first sermon at Sarnath, which explained the Four Noble Truths of the Buddha. The monks in front represent the three original disciples who disputed the Buddha.

of Kapila, a famous Hindu sage, founder of the Samkhya school of philosophy. Samkhya is one of the six classical schools of Hindu philosophy, which were founded to counteract the appeal of Buddhist ideas. That sage, in his anxiety not to upset orthodox hierarchy, had left matters equivocal but the Buddha re-stated the position clearly. What he attempted was not to undertake the impossible task of explaining the origin of the universe but to comprehend the order of its manifestations, as the universe really is.

In the second sermon he preached to the five monks in the deer park at Isipatan at Benares, the Buddha explicitly declared that there is nothing in all the elements which constitutes an individual. 'The body, feeling, perception, consciousness, and all the aggregates are soulless.' The soul may at best be a component thing that represents the synthesis of a totality of our sensations and perceptions but itself cannot be taken as immortal or permanent. In the original Buddhist conception of soul, it is like a mirror of a special kind that does not exist apart from and independent of what it reflects. It comes into being by virtue of what it reflects.

How then, do we reconcile this with a belief in its transmigration? It is logical and much more credible that these references—not consistent with the Buddha's original teachings—were incorporated by the compilers of the Buddhist texts to meet the popular need for reassurance about an afterlife. Some kind of compensation, it seems, had to be offered to ensure compliance with the moral-ethical code. For the Buddha the way itself was the goal—and if one likes—the reward.

The Buddha did not negate all philosophy. He only refuted a particular approach to it. His negations are pregnant with a definite positivistic purpose. He negated the absolute doctrine of the Vedas and brought a breath of fresh air in the stale atmosphere and galvanized Indian thought. What the Buddha affirmed was the principle of causality. This was not entirely new. In both the Yoga and Samkhya systems (Hindu philosophical systems which influenced Buddhist thought), causality has a significant place. According to the Buddha, the principle of causality is allied with the still more important principle of flux of change and becoming. His was one of the earliest formulations of a dynamic view of life. As has been aptly said, he unfolded before humanity vast and fluid horizons—the visions of a universe literally without beginning or end. This was the awakening of a new dawn.

The Buddha's greatness lies in that he never lost his moorings. He taught that because we live in a world of flux, there is all the more reason to cultivate precisely those habits of mind and thought that contribute to tranquility, detachment, poise and peace. He was acutely aware of the squalor and the suffering of the world, its frustrations and misery. His view of life was essentially a compassionate—and a practical—one. He often explained himself with the aid of memorable parables. Once he told a disciple, 'Suppose, a poisoned arrow pierced a man's body and his relatives called a doctor. Now, suppose this man said the arrow should not be pulled out unless I know his name and clan, unless I know whether it was a long bow that he used or a cross bow, unless I know what the bow string was made of, unless I know what the arrow was made of and its feathers, unless I know whether the arrowhead is calf-tooth or razor edge, or barb-headed. Now, all of this may not be discovered and in the meanwhile the man might die. Likewise it is not useful to bother about many things which are not concerned with life as it should be lived. My concern is the suffering in this life and the way to escape suffering.'

The Buddha was against metaphysical speculation. He was quite aware that the reaction against Vedic religion was as much due to the elaborate and expensive sacrificial ritual as due to the abstruse metaphysics of post-Upanishadic thought (the Upanishads were the later Hindu scriptures which constituted a sort of bridge between the Vedic period and Buddhism). Abstract philosophizing and polemic was, he knew, well beyond the reach of the commoner and that metaphysics was an intellectual equivalent of myth. The sophisticated and elaborate system of Buddhist metaphysics, it must be remembered, is the product of the Mahayana school just as the formalized morality and ethics is the creation of the Hinayana school. (Buddhist teachings split into many schools which came to be grouped as the Mahayana or Hinayana schools.)

Facing page: Young monks spend long hours in the class room learning about the scriptures and codes of ethical-moral conduct at the Phodong Monastery (Sikkim).

Orders and Practices

*Through the grace of the guru's
instruction
We have blended creative and
fulfillment meditation.
We have destroyed all distinction
between* samsara *and* nirvana.
*We have united vision and action
in perfect harmony
We know no distinction between
acceptance and rejection.*

*Dwelling in the blessed unity of
vast space and pure awareness,
We know no separation between
self and others.*

Different schools of thought have
branched off to interpret the
noble truths to suit different
psychological temperaments. The
unity of the Sangha—fraternal
community of monks—has
throughout remained intact.

A meeting of monks took place after the Buddha's death (called the first council) and Upali, the barber, presided over it. Anand recited the *Sutta Pitaka,* a collection of aphorisms of Buddha, to authenticate the sermons on ethics. *Sutta Pitaka* is the thread which strings the sayings of the Buddha together. A second council was convened a hundred years after his death when schism raised its head over matters of monastic discipline. The order broke in two, Sthavirvadin (Thervadin in Pali)—meaning those who followed the elders—and the Mahasanghikas, those belonging to the great community. The third council was convened at Pataliputra under King Ashok, which recognized the Sthavirvadins as the orthodox school and expelled the heretics.

The fourth council was held in the reign of Kanishka at which the Sarvastivadin doctrines were codified. By now the difference in interpretation had crystallized to an extent that a split could not be averted. The new ideas developed by the Sarvastivadin and the Mahasanghik led to the division of the Sangha (Order) between Mahayana—the Greater Vehicle, and the Hinayana—the Lesser Vehicle. It was claimed that the Greater Vehicle would carry many more souls to their salvation than the Lesser Vehicle.

Whatever may have been the Buddha's original idea, less than two hundred years after his demise, Buddhism was recognized as a formal religion. In the process, it had borrowed much from the prevalent popular beliefs and practices of the time. According to tradition, *stupas* were constructed at the sites where relics of the Buddha were interred. Of the religious remains between 200 BC and AD 200 those of Buddhist faith far outnumber those of Brahmanism. It is speculated that the Pali canon of the Sthavirvadins originated from the great monastery at Sanchi.

Hinyana and Mahayana Buddhism later branched into four schools. The Hinyana split into two schools, the Vaibhashika (those who accepted the commentaries known as *vibhasha,* written by Buddhist philosopher Katyayaniputra) and the Sautrantika (those who recognised the *Sutras*—the Buddhist cannon—as the sole authority). The Mahayana Buddhism split into the Madhyamika and Yogachara schools. These four schools of thought are the ones which are referred to in various philosophical works dealing with Indian metaphysics.

Hinayana or the Lesser Vehicle

The Sarvastivadins are traced to the Vaibhashika School. It is believed that the Vibhasha commentaries were originally compiled in the second century AD and rendered into Sanskrit by the poet Ashvagosh. Vasubandhu, originally from Gandhara and renowned for his scholarly study of these commentaries, made Kashmir his home. It was from Kashmir that this system of thought was carried to China and its basic

Monks kneel in respect and reverence as the Dalai Lama makes his entry during the Losar festival at Dharamsala (India).

texts were translated into Chinese. The Vaibhashik philosophers are closely identified with Buddhism in Kashmir.

The Sautrantikas emerged as bitter opponents of the Vaibhashik School whom they deplored as realists. As their name indicates, they believed that the *Sutras* (Buddhist canon containing the discourses of the Buddha) were the final authority on matters of philosophical doctrine and no commentaries could be accepted as an alternative. While the Vaibhashikas maintained that the existence of phenomenal objects is based on direct perception, the Sautrantikas asserted that external objects were merely appearances and their existence could only be proved by inference. According to tradition the founder of this school was Kumar Labdha; originally a resident of Taxila.

The Hinayanists, at least for some time, held their own. They too recognized that the times were bad and that secondary goals like residence in heaven or rebirth among gods had to be given due importance. Undeterred by the splendours of Mahayana, the Hinayana scholars devoted themselves to refining the doctrinal implications of *Abhidhamma* (noble or supreme truth).

By the end of the Gupta period (fifth century AD), Buddhism had spread to the different parts of this subcontinent. In Andhra country, the Buddhists had established a strong presence. The *vihar* at Nagarjanikonda, where the great philosopher lived, was discovered only

Monks devote much time in *brahmvihar* (meditation practised in isolation or in a group) as the Buddha laid great emphasis on right contemplation. Meditation helps accomplish an equipoised mind.

in the thirties. Another noted Chinese traveller, Fa-hien's account documents that this site was a flourishing one till the fifth century. The Tamil land, Kanchi, was where Dignag, a Buddhist metaphysician, lived. In Kathiawar, Valabhi was a famous Buddhist centre. Ajanta and Ellora fall in the present day Maharashtra and show that Buddhism was popular in this region. Many *stupas* were constructed and the *vihars* were richly endowed. These were located at Amaravati, Junnar, Karle and Kanheri.

Hinayana could not long compete with the popular appeal of Mahayana and disappeared from the land of its birth but, carried beyond India's shores, it struck strong roots in Burma, Ceylon, Thailand, Laos and Vietnam.

After the Gupta period there was a general decline in social and cultural life and Indian religion became permeated with ideas of sympathetic magic and sexual mysticism. Buddhism could not remain untouched by these trends for long.

Mahayana or the Greater Vehicle

The founder of the Madhyamika school is the famous philosopher Nagarjuna, a Brahmin from the Deccan. According to his teachings, the phenomenal world is a misconceived superimposition on Reality and it

Hand gestures have special symbolic significance in Buddhism. Manipulation of ritual objects like the *dorje-vajra* (diamond sceptre) forms an integral part of daily monastic routine in Tibetan Buddhism.

is absolutely wrong to make a distinction between the world (*samsara*) and Reality *(sunyata)* .

Madhyamika means the middle doctrine and should not be confused with the middle way preached by the Buddha. Nagarjuna concentrated on pairs of polar opposites like unity and diversity, annihilation and permanence and sought to clarify that nothing ultimately meaningful could be expressed by these. The mystical middle ground is what comprised *sunyata,* which is commonly translated as void. Reality, he taught lies in this middle domain—between the extremes.

The concept of *sunyata* is propounded in the *Garland of Flowers,* an important part of the Buddhist cannon, composed in the third century AD. This mystical work is devoted to the problem of understanding the essential nature of the universe—*thatata. Thatata* is used in Mahayana Buddhism to explain the ultimate and unconditioned nature of all things. If expressed positively, it can be called *sunyata* as it can only be understood by realizing that one can neither find it by searching nor lose it by trying to separate oneself from it. According to Nagarjuna, phenomena are the ocean considered as waves; the essential nature is the waves considered as the ocean. The metaphysic of void—*sunyata—*

Following page 52: Monks were expected to lead a wandering life and were only allowed refuge during the monsoon. With the passage of time many of these hermitages became permanent dwellings for monks.

is worked out in great detail. *Sunyata*, it should be noted, does not preclude qualified practical reality. With the passage of time, the concept of *sunyata* became *prajna parmita*—a kind of revealed truth or transcendental wisdom.

The founder of the other Mahayana sect, the Yogachara school is believed to be Maitreyanath who lived in Ayodhya and composed many works systematizing the idealistic stream in Buddhist thought. Many subtle and different shades of philosophical beliefs evolved within this school. The most famous thinker in this school is perhaps Asanga from Peshawar. He is credited with outlining the detailed practices prescribed for a Yogachari adept. It is believed that Asanga converted his younger brother Vasubandhu, who was a famous Sarvastivadin, to become a Yogachari.

Madhyamika thinkers were primarily concerned with the intellectual investigation of reality, the Yogacharis focussed their attention on the psychological dimension of life and strove to gain insights through meditation. Their conclusion was that all things that are real are undifferentiated and this essential unity may be experienced directly though meditation.

The Yogachara school is also associated with the poet, Ashvagosh, and other metaphysicians who developed it, like Dignag and Shilbhadra in the fifth and sixth centuries. They evolved a notion of the subconscious stratum of phenomena or the 'store-consciousness' which underlies all human consciousness, called *alay vijana*. This school greatly influenced Chinese and Tibetan Buddhism. Hieun Tsang, the great Chinese traveller to India, studied under Shilbhadra and wrote a book on the metaphysical school of Yogachara.

The Madhyamikas were bitterly opposed by the Yogacharis. The fundamental assertion made by the Yogachari philosophers was that everything is just the manifestation of a universal mind. There can be no question of a subject/object duality. Any such presumption is *maya*. It is from this concept of *maya* that the Hindu philosopher Sankara is believed to have developed his philosophy of the Advait (monism) which does not distinguish between individual self and cosmic reality.

Without going into confusing detail it may be noted that during the days of its greatest vitality, Buddhist centres of learning encouraged a healthy debate and no effort was made to stifle the voice of dissent. It can also be seen that the rival schools of thought coexisted not only in monastic universities but also within the same family. While one teacher-thinker or his school may have been predominant in a region, the stimulating ideas recognized no geographical barrier. The community

Previous page 53: The Bodhi tree which sheltered the young ascetic, Siddharth, and under which he attained Enlightenment provides shade and comfort to pilgrims in the compound of the temple at Bodhgaya.

Facing page: Boddhisattva Avalokiteshvara—the compassionate one—is shown here holding a lotus flower: Ajanta. The concept of *boddhisattva*—he who delays his own deliverance to assist suffering humanity—is essential to the Mahayana doctrine.

These statues from Ellora (India) provide a glimpse of the great variety in which the Buddha's image has been rendered. Even when hewn in stone, the human body seems to retain a pulsating plasticity.

of monks formed a lively, intellectual brotherhood and the cross-fertilization of ideas contributed to intellectual sophistication. Despite the splitting of the Buddhist Sangha into many different branches, Buddhism continued to flourish in the land of its birth and when Hieun-Tsang visited India in the seventh century AD, he estimated that the number of Hinyana and Mahayana monks was almost equal—about one hundred and twenty thousand monks each.

It also cannot be overlooked that increasing fascination with abstraction and obtuse logic distanced the philosophers from the common man. It was not only due to the assault of the armies of Islam that Buddhism vanished from the land of its birth but also this increasingly confusing metaphysics and sectarian schisms that dealt a mortal blow to the noble religion.

On the one hand the faithful were drawn towards the incarnate gods borrowed from Hinduism, on the other they felt attracted by the compelling charms and quasi-magical practices of Tantra (Vajrayana Buddhism). Many historians believe that the decline of Buddhism coincided with the weakening of the rational tradition and emergence

Previous pages 56-57: The usually reticent monks caught in an exuberant mood against the backdrop of colourful prayer flags, during the festival of Losar, the Tibetan New Year.

Many of the Ellora cave shrines frame beautiful Buddha statues with colourful paintings dramatically enhancing the visual impact.

of occult and esoteric practices. However, it can be argued with equal validity that the abstruse philosophical speculations enfeebled the spirit of rationalism.

In the early days the teachings of the Buddha were conveyed to the common man without any barrier, in easy-to-understand folk idiom. The middle way was pragmatic and practicable. When scholasticism became its hallmark, what the academicians and the learned monks considered rational and logical became irrelevant for the prince and the peasant alike. It has been argued Mahayana Buddhism emerged to sustain the faith of the masses when Hinyana was beginning to dry up and failing to hold interest and Vajrayana made its appearance when Mahayana's hold was weakening. Unfortunately the tantric practices in Buddhism as in Hinduism soon degenerated into esoteric ritual and superstition. It has been aptly remarked that the doctrinal debates carried within themselves the seeds of their destruction.

The Buddhist metaphysical exertions deeply influenced the evolution of brahmanical-Vedantic (relating to the Vedanta, or 'end of the Vedas' school) philosophy. Vasubandhu—a brother of Asanga—refuted in a masterly fashion the existence of the external world and upheld the reality of *vijnana*. *Vijnana* is the consciousness which is below the threshold of normal experience or the subliminal consciousness. In order to explain the non-reality of the external world, the concerned

Ritual Objects and Forms of Worship

It is by capturing the essential relationship between monastic life (and discipline) and liturgical ritual objects, that the overall picture of Buddhist worship emerges.

Of the constituents of ceremonial worship, the chant is the *geeta* (melody) element—sonorous sound that tunes the mind to a milieu of contemplative reflection. The *mantra*—mystic

A Buddhist monk in meditation.

syllables in a special sequence—may not have any linguistic meaning but they are believed to be charged with potential energy and have great evocative power. Incense (*dhoop*) exudes *sugandha* or aroma, that invites and gently overpowers the sense of smell and does not allow the mind to stray or be enticed by other odours. *Naivedya*, the offering of food relates to the sense of taste; *dipa*, the lamp, contributes light which dispels darkness and allows us to see clearly. *Pushpa*, flowers, soft to touch, involve yet another sense organ. The whole idea is to orchestrate perception to the heightening of consciousness and the experiencing of the sublime. *Arghyam* is the pure drinking water and *padyam* is cool water for washing the feet. *Gandha* is the perfumed water for anointing; and *shabda* the cymbal.

The inspiration for these forms of worship seems to come from Hindu offerings, which are sixteen in number and share common elements with the Buddhist way. For example,

A young incarnate lama in his ceremonial regalia.

flowers, incense, the lamp and offering of food are used in Hindu worship. And besides the offerings during worship, the other items on the altar are a miniature *chaitya-stupa*, one or more sacred books, a sceptre *(dorje)*, which is a symbolic counterpart of the bell used in Hindu worship, a vase containing holy water, a large mirror, the divine arrow, two pairs of cymbals, a conch shell, a pair of human thighbone trumpets, a human skull drum and rosaries.

61

Buddhism has returned to India with the influx of a large population of Tibetan refugees. Followers of the Dalai Lama belonging to the Yellow Hat sect strive hard to keep their traditional festivals alive in exile: Dharamsala.

Buddhist text compares it to the horns of the hare, the son of a barren woman, and the circle of fire produced when a burning stick is twirled around. These images loom large in the development of the Advait or monist philosophy.

One of the most important innovations of the Mahayana school was the introduction of the *trikaya* doctrine of the three bodies of the Buddha (the *dharmakaya*, the *sambhogkaya* and the *nirmankaya*). The Mahayanists followed the Mahasangkhikas of the second council in minimizing the importance of the historical Buddha. The Buddha, according to this doctrine, abides for aeons and preaches the law at different times in countless places, in innumerable garbs. *Dharmakaya* is the essential nature, *sambhogkaya* is the blissful body in which Buddha manifests himself in the heavens, and *nirmankaya* is the body he assumes on earth for the benefit of mortals. The great Mahayana text, *Diamond Sutra,* tells this in a famous verse:

Those who follow my form did see me,
And those who followed me by voice,
Wrong the efforts they engaged in,
Me those people will not see!
From the Dhamma body should one see the Buddha,
From the Dhamma body comes their guidance.

Radong, an ornate long horn trumpet is an important accessory in Tibetan Buddhist ritual. Its pure sound seems to resound forever.

The Mahayanists were not content even with this. They sought to link the historical Buddha by a number of mythological fictions to their own concept. They claimed that the council at Rajgriha which codified the Hinayana *Sutras* was paralleled by a council on Mount Vimalsvabhav, where an assembly of Bodhisattvas (those who come to this earth as Buddha to relieve suffering) had codified the *Sutra* for Mahayanists. According to Nagarjuna, five hundred years after the Buddha's Nirvana when the good law after having gradually declined was in great danger, these treasures from the past were rediscovered and revealed to revivify the doctrine.

The main feature of Mahayana Buddhism is the shift of emphasis on the goal from the *arhat* (saint) to the Bodhisattva ideal, and the ranking of compassion on the same plane as wisdom, which has six stages or *parmitas.* The concept of Bodhisattva is an important one in the Mahayana sect. Bodhisattva is a personage who has postponed his own *nirvana* until the rest of suffering humanity is not liberated from the distressing cycle of rebirth. Not all Bodhisattvas attain Buddhahood. Sakyamuni is the name given to Siddharth Gautam who, according to this doctrine, is only the most recent in a long chain of Buddhas who have appeared on earth to deliver mankind from torment. Among the most popular Bodhisattvas are Avalokiteshvara Padmapani, the most compassionate one; Manjushri, the destroyer of ignorance and error; and Maitreya, who is also believed to be a future Buddha.

According to the Mahayana belief, a Bodhisattva bides his time till the smallest insect has secured its salvation. The universe of the Great Vehicle contains many Bodhisattvas. Apart from the ones mentioned above, there are also Vajrapani, the stern foe of sin, and Ksitigarbha, the guardian of purgatories.

Not content with creating the pantheon of Bodhisattvas, the Mahayanists also conceived of a host of female deities. Female deities are the embodiment of the potency of their consorts: *Prajna parmita* is the perfection of insight. *Matangis* were outcaste women, *pishachis* the demonesses, she-ghouls; *dakinis,* sorceresses; *yoginis,* saviouresses. Magical symbols or *yantra,* magical formulae *or mantra,* and *sadhana* or disciplined practice for becoming an adept, formed the core of Buddhist Tantrism which symbolizes that the basic quality of manifestation is composed of some deity or aspect of Reality, with a female partner locked in sexual embrace.

While the Lesser Vehicle taught that release from *dukha* or unhappiness is obtained by the gradual loss of individuality, the Greater Vehicle held out the hope that the process could be accelerated and assisted by compassionate Bodhisattvas.

The Bodhisattva—literally, essence of enlightenment—tries to get rid of the ego by active self-sacrifice and selfless service, cognitive by insight into the objective non-existence of a self. The first is due to compassion, the second to wisdom. A Bodhisattva remains in touch with common people and shares their passions but these do not taint his mind.

Mahayana Buddhism concentrated on the liberation of the masses, not the individual. That is why it is called the Greater Vehicle; it could be used by many in sharp contrast with Hinayana, the smaller or the inferior vehicle. The Mahayana met with the requirements of the laity and gained in popularity. In due course Mahayana spread to Nepal, Tibet, Mongolia, China, Korea and Japan.

Tantric Buddhism

The Vehicle of the Thunderbolt—Vajrayana—made its appearance in the eighth century in eastern India. This is the sect which established itself as the dominant faith in Tibet. This was accomplished largely through the exertions of the missionaries dispatched from the monastery at Vikramshila. The Vajrayanis offered the short cut of magical practices. This sect developed after AD 1000 in Tibet, imbibing influences from both India and China and retaining a core of pre-Buddhist Bon beliefs which were essentially shamanistic, involving nature-worship, with psychic and sexual practices. It sought to amalgamate the tradition of

Facing page: The Rizong monastery in Ladakh. The remote location of these monasteries in the rugged trans-Himalayan region protected them from vandals, and therefore many of them survived intact.

Dalai Lama

The Dalai Lama, also known as the *Gyalwa Rimpoche* (that translates as the 'Precious Protector') is considered to be the embodiment of enlightenment and perfection. The protector is, above all, a teacher, one who shows his followers the path. What creates some confusion is that the person who is occupying the office of the Dalai Lama is at the same time an incarnation of his predecessor—the successor to a celestial dynasty and also a mortal human being. He is not like God, supreme and unapproachable. He is, in fact, the embodiment of the *bodhisattva* ideal. To appreciate his role in the life of Tibet and his significance as the most revered Buddhist monk, it is necessary to review the birth and evolution of the institution.

The Dalai Lama, the head of the Yellow Hat Gelugpa sect, has contributed a great deal towards conveying the essence of Buddhism to the contemporary world.

In the fourteenth century, a Tibetan monk, Tsong Khapa, reformed Tibetan Buddhism with great zeal and established a new Gelugpa sect (that became famous as the 'Yellow Hats' due to their distinctive headgear). It was Sonam Gyatso, the third 'pope' in this sect, who received the title of Dalai Lama from the Mongolian ruler Altan Khan. The word *dalai* in Mongolian means ocean, and the honorific was a tribute to the vast knowledge of the king's spiritual preceptor.

The fifth Dalai Lama won fame as a military commander and brought about the secular unification of Tibet. He was also an astute diplomat and secured Tibet's independence by maintaining a delicate balance between the two powerful neighbours—the Mongols and the Chinese.

It was the fifth Dalai Lama who referred to his tutor as *panchen*. *Panchen* is the hybrid abbreviation of two words—*pandit* and *chenpo*—meaning, scholar and great, respectively. It was this lama who built the famous monastery at Tashilunpo in AD 1445 which became the seat of the Panchen Lama, who acquired great political power in the eighteenth century. It was not long before the Chinese started playing one Tibetan Lama against the other and subverted the country's independence. The Cheng emperors made the Panchen Lama the ruler of Tsang in western Tibet.

Of the many remarkable Dalai Lamas, the sixth has been controversial for being known as a man given to a life of pleasure, a writer of romantic verses in youth. He was eventually assassinated. The seventh Dalai Lama, in contrast, was recognized as a saint in his lifetime. In the meantime, the Chinese authorities argued that while the Dalai Lama was the spiritual head of the Tibetan people, Panchen Lama wielded political power. Several Dalai Lamas (from the eighth to the twelfth) died young in the midst of conspiracy, intrigue and political designs over Tibet.

By the beginning of this century, Tibet was criss-crossed by imperial rivalries

One of the most onerous tasks of abbots and senior monks is to identify and test the reincarnation of a future lama before confirming the succession.

involving Russia, China and Great Britain. The thirteenth Dalai Lama issued a declaration of Tibetan independence and attempted social reforms. When he died in 1937, it was generally recognized that his contribution to the Tibetan people was substantial. Then, events went against the fate of the country; and after the civil war in China and the communists coming to power, Tibet came under severe pressure.

The present Dalai Lama (the fourteenth), Tenzing Gyasto, was driven into exile in 1959, when the Chinese 'liberated' Tibet amidst violence. Henceforth the role of the Dalai Lama became greatly politicized. He, besides being the spiritual leader, is also the symbol of Tibetan people's dissent and protest against oppression. The Nobel Peace Prize awarded to him is a token of the esteem he is held in, worldwide. The fourteenth Dalai Lama's exiled home is at the Dharamsala, in India, a place singularly identified with the Tibetan refugee community and its spiritual-political leader.

hathyoga—harnessing of the physical body for a spiritual purpose—and *tantra* or esoteric ritual. The Tibetan *tangkhas* (Buddhist scroll paintings), in this sense, are much more than examples of religious art, they are priceless repositories of information about the evolution of Vajrayana doctrines in Tibet.

Mandala, an important element of Vajrayana Buddhism, is a diagrammatic representation of cosmic forces in a mythological personified form. Symbols express primordial influences and fears. Microcosm and macrocosm are equated, reproducing the drama of the universe in each individual's mind. The human body is viewed as a *mandala* with a rough and ready correspondence established between the five elements and the five *chakras* (centres). The *chakras* are co-related with the five elements, fire, water, air, ether and earth. *Mandalas* are specially important in the Vajrayana sect that sought to impose order on the chaotic explosion of ideas and assumption.

Feminine deities play an important role in Vajrayana Buddhism and are referred to as *prajnas* (wisdom) and *vidyas* (knowledge). Prominent among these are Tara and Prajnaparmita. In addition, there are the *dakinis* or sorceresses. They play a crucial role in the esoteric ritual of Tantrayana. This sect of Buddhism shows some features similar to *hathyoga* but it would be wrong to confuse *tantric* practices in Hinduism and Buddhism. Tibetan masters, like the yogi-poet Milerapa, were founders of a strong, original mystical tradition and made valuable contributions to the Vajrayana stream.

The five Dhyani Buddhas who are abstractions or mind pictures magically correspond to the five-fold division of the cosmic forces. The identifications follow transformations and transfigurations linking all forces and facts of the universe to these Tathagatas. These are like archetypal images that emerge from the subconscious. Mara, the evil tempter, for instance, personifies the negative components of human personality like *klesha* (sorrow) and *mrityu* (mortality).

Kashmir, Gandhara and Afghanistan continued to be the strongholds of Hinayana Buddhism till the fifth century AD. Vasubandhu was the most powerful exponent of the Sarvastivadin philosophy. His *Abhidhammakosha* was recognized as the authoritative exposition of this metaphysics. The Muslim invasion of India forced many Buddhist monks to flee to Nepal and Kashmir. The influx of refugees failed to reinvigorate the enfeebled faith. Instead, a wonderful fusion of Buddhism and Shaivism took place in Kashmir during the eighth to the thirteenth centuries.

Facing page: Training in monastic life begins early for most Buddhist monks. Many join the Sangha in early adolescence. Young novitiates spend most of their time studying the scriptures.
Following pages 70-71: The multi-tiered Baudha in Kathmandu (Nepal) provides a spectacular example of 'evolved' stupa architecture—from a simple funerary receptacle marked by a heap of stones to an elaborate and inspiring edifice.

Many scholars went to the trans-Himalayan region and won many new converts. Ladakh, Spiti and Gughe became important centres of Buddhist scholarship. Shakyasribhadra was a Kashmiri scholar who went to Tibet. Muslim rule reached Kashmir in 1339. At first it was tolerant of Buddhism. But soon persecutions began, temples and monasteries were destroyed and Buddhism in this region could never recover from this brutal blow.

The conquest of Kathmandu valley by the Gurkhas in 1768 reduced the Buddhist Newars to a minority and accelerated the process of decay. A number of deities began to be worshipped in the manner of Hindu gods. These were seen as powerful saviours, not compassionate Bodhisattvas or path-finding masters. The popular cults blurred the dividing line between Buddhism and Hinduism. In many cases the same image is worshipped by those professing different faiths.

After AD 1000 the picture presented is one of accelerated decline. The manuscripts suffered. Their condition tells a sorry tale. The quality of art also declined sharply. Vows of celibacy among monks were not observed and finally given up. The monks started to bring their families to the *vihar*. Only the outward form of the religion survived.

Buddhist monasteries are no longer grottoes in the rock. The life prescribed for the monk may be spartan but many monasteries like Rumtek are housed in richly painted and comfortably furnished buildings.

Buddhism beyond Indian Borders

Why has misfortune befallen us?
Why has the Buddha's doctrine
failed us?
Why are the powers of darkness
rising?
Why have evil storm clouds eclipsed
The whiteness of the moon, the
compassion of Mahakarunika?
Is my holy guru, the Indestructible
Diamond,
Falling prey to decay and death?
Evil portents have driven me here.
I pray you, bestow upon us
Your compassionate grace.

Potala—a unique combination of a
fort-palace and a shrine—perched
atop a hill commands a breathtaking
view of Lhasa. The traditional
residence of the Dalai Lama, it is a
quintessential symbol of Tibet.

The teachings of the Buddha not only spread steadily throughout the length of India but also travelled well beyond its borders to distant lands and took roots there. In several countries Buddhism is still the dominant religion and at other places its cultural imprint is indelible.

Tibet-China, Nepal, Bhutan and Burma are adjacent to the Indian landmass and naturally experienced the impact of the invigorating thought before others, as it radiated from the great centres of Buddhist scholarship in Bengal and Bihar. Taxila in the north-western frontier was an equally famous stronghold of Buddhist philosophy and culture and played a significant role in the transmission of Buddhist thought in the central Asian region. A great deal was accomplished due to the exertions of missionary scholars embarking from Kashmir. The two streams from India-Nepal and Turkestan-Mongolia converged in Tibet resulting in a wonderful synthesis.

The island kingdoms of Sri Lanka and Indonesia encountered Buddhism through intrepid seafaring traders and missionaries in the centuries before and after the birth of Christ. Siam—modern Thailand—and Cambodia on mainland Southeast Asia did not remain untouched for long. With time, Mongolia, Japan and Korea came under the sway of Buddhism.

In **China,** there was some resistance to the imported ideas to begin with but the new faith soon overcame this prejudice. The rise of Buddhism coincided with the revival of Taoism in China and many Chinese saw and stressed the similarity between the two intellectual trends. Buddhism seemed to supplement Taoism uniquely and provided something which indigenous teachers were looking for.

Soon Buddhism in China spawned different schools of thought, of which two finally emerged as pre-eminent. These were Amidism and C'han. Amidism drew inspiration from the Bodhisattva Amitabh and derived its name from him. The emphasis was on the devotional aspect stressed in the Mahayana school. C'han is related to the original Sanskrit word *dhyan* which means contemplative meditation. Those belonging to this school believed that there resides a Buddha in each individual's heart and this self-realization leads to liberation from suffering.

Although we find frequent references to five main streams of Chinese Buddhism, the two that can be distinctly identified are Tsao-tsungitsung and Lin-chi-I-hsuan. The first lays emphasis on silent meditation, and its teachings are closely rooted in the *Chinese Book of Changes*—the *I-ching*. The second favours the 'shout and stick' or the shock therapy approach to awaken the pupil and to impart insights or spiritual illumination.

Scholars believe that the neo-Confucian renaissance in China owes a great deal to the contributions of C'han Buddhists. Magnificent C'han monasteries were established under the patronage of the Sung emperors and became the focal points of social and cultural life.

The C'han monks encouraged the tradition of the Kung-An. Kung-An is a riddle or a paradox which is meant to trigger off a breakthrough—remove a mental block—and pave the way for spiritually liberating self-realisation. This is the origin of the Zen Koan. As one Buddhist master put it, 'One must persist with the practice of Kung-An diligently, you must not let go of the problem for a single moment, let your attention be fixed upon the riddle without interruption, when you begin to tire and lose interest that is when extra caution has to be exercised, you must know it is the final moment approaching, do not let it slip out of your grasp. A sudden flash of light will illuminate the entire face of the universe, the land of the fully enlightened will be fully revealed to you at the point of a single hair and you will be able to see the wheel of dharma revolving in a single grain of sand.'

Buddhism reached **Japan** via China and the Buddhist deities soon established peace with the pre-existing Shinto gods. The Japanese responded warmly to C'han concepts and it was in the 'land of the rising sun' that the Zen Buddhism blossomed gloriously. During the Samurai (noble warrior) period, violent death was a fact of everyday life and the average Japanese concerned with death was very rare. A Samurai was a member of the feudal warrior class of Japan which was bound by the code of bushido, emphasizing qualities of loyalty, bravery, and endurance. It seems that the popularity of Zen owes a great deal to its promise of liberating its practitioners from the fear of death. Zen emphasizes actions that are simple and uncomplicated, but have great depth and elegance. What is astonishing is that Zen became equally popular among the noble warrior elite and the peasants.

Zen Buddhism in Japan stimulated great creativity in calligraphy, painting, art and architecture, and for a period of about a thousand years remained the dominant influence in Japan's cultural life. It was only around AD 1500 that with the drying up of political patronage Japanese Buddhism began to lose its creative inspirational momentum. Under the Japanese emperor Tokugawa, during the cult of Shogunate (Shogun was the hereditary commander of the army in feudal Japan) Zen Buddhism was at its weakest. Because of the military power concentrated in his hands, and the consequent weakness of the nominal head of state, the Shogun was generally the real ruler of the country until feudalism was abolished in 1867. There was a resurgence of Confucianism and Shintoism in Tokugawa's reign which relegated Buddhism to the background. It was only towards the end of the nineteenth century that there was a revival of interest in Buddhism and today, the interest in Zen Buddhism is widespread throughout the world.

On the mainland southeast Asia, Burma, Thailand and Laos are recognised as Buddhist countries. The form of Buddhism prevailing in this region is Thervada/Hinyana Buddhism. Buddhism in **Burma** has enjoyed a more or less uninterrupted dominance since the eleventh century when King Anawartha of the Pagan dynasty drove out the priests belonging to the Vajarayana sect and imported some priests of his choice from Sri Lanka. After the fall of Pagan dynasty at the hands of the Mongol hordes of Kublai Khan, the country suffered five hundred years of strife and Buddhist influence diminished a little. The pre-Buddhist spirits (*nats*) reappeared and to this date enjoy undiminished popularity. However the Buddhist Sangha remained in close contact with the rural populace and

Following pages 78-79: The famous Golden Rock in Burma in Kyaik-to. The shrine is built on a gold-plated boulder atop a cliff and according to legend, the precarious balance is maintained by a hair of the Buddha preserved in the pagoda.

the chief means of acquiring merit became the building of a pagoda. The popularity of Buddhism in Burma is demonstrated by the remnants of nine thousand pagodas which once filled an area of approximately fifteen kilometres in Pagan. Amongst the most famous Buddhist shrines is the Anand temple built in the eleventh century where the 547 *Jataka* tales are pictorially represented on glazed plaques. The coming of the British in 1885 dealt a severe blow to the central ecclesiastical authority but this did not inhibit the monks from playing an important role in the anti-colonial freedom struggle of Burma. It is remarkable that while the Burmese Buddhists have remained orthodox in doctrinal matters in the domain of politics, theirs has been the most courageous voice of dissent. The resistance offered by the Buddhist monks and the pupils has focussed international attention on the oppressive military rule in that country. Buddhism in Burma has also reduced ethnic rivalries and made a substantial contribution to the cultural life of that country.

Buddhism is the state religion in **Thailand** and even the monarchs there traditionally spend some time at least as ordained monks in a monastery. The architectural inheritance is predominantly Buddhist and a unique amalgam of Hindu-Buddhist legend and lore is witnessed in the classic/epic and the folk tradition. It is believed that Buddhism was transmitted to **Cambodia,** 'the land of the Khmers' from Thailand. In Cambodia too, it was this fusion of Buddhist and Hindu ideas and iconography that became popular and imbibed a lot of indigenous influences. The majestic monuments at Angkor Wat are adorned with the most impressive Buddhist imagery. In **Indonesia,** Tantric Buddhism was dominant until it was suppressed in the fourteenth century by Islam. The grand stupa at Borobudur in central **Java** remains an impressive testimony to the past glory of Buddhism in this land. It is designed as a cosmic *mandala* rendered architecturally. It is believed that a circumambulation of this shrine imparts greatest merit. The island kingdom of **Sri Lanka** and the peninsular empire in Indonesia adopted Buddhism enthusiastically and today one encounters local versions with a distinct personality of their own. In Sri Lanka, Buddhism continues to be a living faith more than 2,400 years after it was first introduced. The Mauryan emperor, Ashok, despatched a royal mission to Sri Lanka and the various Chinese travellers have testified to Buddhism's popularity in the first millennium AD. Proximity with India made it possible for Sri Lankans to make frequent pilgrimages and carry on a lively scholarly exchange on theological issues. Tradition maintains that Buddhaghosh, a brahmin from Gaya, composed in Anuradhapur, a famous text *Vishudhimagga*, expounding the doctrine of *shila* (conduct), *samadhi* (contemplation) and *prajna* (wisdom), as also commentaries on the three *pitakas*, the Buddhist texts. Sri Lanka also played an important role in communicating and reinforcing Buddhist ideas to other countries in the Far East. Sri Lanka possesses many archaeological sites of great beauty and historical significance.

Facing page: Buddhist pilgrims from foreign lands have come for centuries to India to revivify the faith. Rajgir is a popular site for devotees from East Asia, who have helped construct many religious monuments here.

Art and Iconography

*I mould the leather of preconcep-
tion and conceptual thought
Around the last of emptiness and
compassion.
Taking the awl of intuitive insight,
I stitch with a thread of existence
That knows no beginning and no
end. Spontaneously,
Freed of the eight mundane obses-
sions,
I create fine slippers of
Dharmakaya.*

Brilliantly coloured images of the
Buddha, of *bodhisattvas* and *siddhas*
(the enlightened one, the
compassionate advisors and the
adepts) adorn the walls of
monasteries. They are not merely
decorative, but also inspirational and
aid meditation.

The contemplation of the beautiful according to the Buddha's own teachings makes us free from selfishness and leads us to the plane of perfect harmony. Sublimities of art inspire us to strive ceaselessly for liberation. Art, as Lama Anagrika Govinda, the famous German Buddhist born in 1898 as E. L. Hoffmann, so perceptively points out, serves as 'the lens that focalizes the rays of an illuminating sun'. The truly beautiful is the truly meaningful as it lights up our life. It not only establishes an intimate relationship between man and his surroundings but also transcends his momentary existence. It ends his separateness and enables him to become contemplative. The beautiful, as the lama emphasizes, does not exclude the terrible or the terrifying. The rhythm of Eastern art, as some Western scholars have suggested, is not of rational origin. It follows an inner rhythm like that of music. It is not surprising that Buddhists value art as a meditative practice. What we must remember is that it is not the subject of art that decides its value but rather the inspirational impetus that it provides to the beholder.

Sculpture and Architecture

The earliest examples of Buddhist art are the Ashokan edicts inscribed on monolithic stone pillars decorated with an animal capital. These are found in all parts of India with the exception of the far south. These comprise the first important group of stone sculptures in the country. The lion capital from Sarnath has been adopted by independent India as its state emblem. Another well known relic is the bull capital from Rampurva in Bihar that now adorns the President of India's house. The beauty of these objects makes us think that crowning animals must have been the product of a long tradition of erecting pillars and carving animal figures, maybe in metal. These show a remarkable similarity with the animal sculptures from the Indus valley.

Ashok is also credited with the excavation of a number of small rock shrines near Bodhgaya and construction of many a *stupa*—a quintessentially Buddhist monument. Buddhist scriptures say that the Buddha's remains were divided and structures were raised over them. The *stupas* then house the relics of Buddha and other Buddhist saints. It has also been suggested that the pillars in a *stupa* represent the cosmic axis of the world—the axis *mundi*. These continue to be objects of most fervent worship in Burma and Sri Lanka.

The earliest *stupa* to have survived in India is the one at Bharhut in Madhya Pradesh. It is dated to the second century BC. Small reliefs from the *stupa* railings depict scenes from the life of the Buddha as recounted in the *Jatakas*. Buddha himself is represented only symbolically. This provides an example of Buddhist iconography in its infancy though some of the illustrations have a quaint charm of their own. The *yakshas* (demi-gods) and gods like *surya* (sun-god)

The lion capital from an Ashokan pillar at Sarnath has been adopted as the national emblem of independent India.

The gateways *(toran)* at Sanchi mark the four cardinal points. The *vedika* (railings) around the *stupa* are richly decorated with illustrations from the *Jataka* tales.

demonstrate the extent to which pre-Buddhist elements were incorporated in Buddhist art.

The next stage is marked by the *stupa* at Sanchi built in the first century after the birth of Christ—the most splendid of all the surviving Indian *stupas*. Its only rival in abundance and surpassing quality of sculpture was perhaps the great *stupa* at Amaravati (Andhra Pradesh) constructed in the Satavahana period but unfortunately nothing remains of this majestic monument now. However, the *toran* (decorated gateways) and *vedika* (surrounding railings) at Sanchi are in a superb state of preservation. Although even here the Buddha is not shown in a human form, the cross bars are decorated with a profusion of human images shown against their natural background. It is a marvellous combination of close observation and sophisticated composition for didactic purposes.

Early monuments at Sanchi, Bharhut and Bodhgaya are mostly funerary structures. The *stupa* is primarily a receptacle for relics of the Buddha or other *arhats* (saints). Many of these structures stand on a rectangular base with axial approaches on four sides. Dhammeka Stupa at Sarnath is 128 feet high. The spherical burial mound is encircled by a *vedika*—railing reminiscent of the transition from wood to stone architecture with *toran* as an ornamented gateway. Both the *vedika* and *toran* are covered with carvings depicting episodes in the Buddha's life. Most of these illustrations are inspired by the *Jataka* tales.

An interesting feature of these sculptures is that the Buddha at first is represented only through symbols like a lotus, a footprint, a caparisoned horse, the *bodhi* tree under which he attained enlightenment, the *stupa,* or the Wheel of Law. It is only at Amaravati around the second century AD that the Buddha is represented in human form.

Chaitya, the other typical Buddhist structure, can be traced back to a word that means 'heaping up'. In its real Buddhist sense, it means a sacred mound. Applied in the complete context, it signifies a hall that contains a *stupa. Chaitya* has characteristic architectural features— facades, and arches or *gavakshas.* Reproduced in miniature, these became common features of Hindu temples in later centuries. The most astonishing specimen of a Buddhist *chaitya* is the one at Karle (in Maharashtra). Here one can also see the actual wood elements of an earlier architectural style surviving and blending with stone work. The interior of the Karle *chaitya* is regarded as the supreme achievement of the early cave temple form.

Icons and Imagery

Some of the most beautiful Buddha images come from Gandhara. Gandhara comprised the rolling plains watered by the river Kabul down to the Indus, south of Muree hills. Taxila, near the present day Islamabad (capital of Pakistan) situated at the crossroads of the historic silk route, was a great centre of Buddhist learning. Most of the Gandhara statues are those of the Buddha himself.

Early Buddhist iconography drew heavily upon Hindu models. The Buddha in the Gandhara style is shown standing or seated replete with the *lakshana* (signs) of a *mahapurush*—great man—and the rendering reflects the blending of religious and aesthetic elements from diverse sources. The Western elements are dominant in the style: the treatment of the robe is classical and even the emaciated features of the Buddha follow the stylization typical to the image of Christ. The garment is treated in the typically Graeco-Roman manner, the heavy folds have a plastic interest of their own, the head appears modelled on Apollo.

The Gandhara Buddha is at once a monk without a tonsure and a prince bereft of his jewellery. He is seldom shown with a begging bowl in his hand. Almost invariably the hands are held in a symbolic

Facing page: Young Siddharth attired as a prince before he renounced the world. This statue, an excellent specimen of the Gandhara style, shows distinct Hellenistic influence.

ritual gesture, the *mudra*. There is a cranial protuberance and elongated ears perhaps due to the earrings.

Besides the Buddha, we come across many Bodhisattvas. They are depicted wearing a variety of ornaments and their hair is ornately arranged. The most striking image is that of the Maitreya from Gandhara with a jar of nectar held in his hand.

Other regional schools of sculpture also produced wonderful statues of the Buddha in a distinct style of their own and are parts of the priceless heritage of Indian art. Mathura and Sarnath Buddhas are no less impressive than the Gandhara ones. Only it seems that the Gandhara style with its Western resonance appealed more to the pioneering Western scholars in this field.

The Buddha image in Sarnath is, it has been noted by scholars, absolutely independent of the Gandhara school. It reveals in full glory the characteristic Indian genius of being able to carve out a figure in perfect harmony with its spiritual conception. By the Gupta period, even the Gandhara Buddhas in terracotta were Indianised and barely show any foreign influence. The Buddha image was rendered with beautiful curly hair, while the Kushana type had a shaven head. Graceful ornamentation was added. The effect of the drapery in earlier Gandhara art had been to display the charms of the flesh and now it became a veil. The spiritual expression, the tranquil smile and the serene, contemplative mood show the triumph of the artiste—the challenge of portraying a celestial being personifying highest wisdom and boundless compassion was not an easy task.

Postures and *Gestures*

The Buddha statues illustrate various postures and gestures—*asanas* and *mudras. Asanas* are the different postures in which the Buddha is portrayed in the images. The standing posture is called *sthanak,* and the seated posture is *asana.* The reclining pose is the *shayan. Mudras* signify protection from fear or *abhay; dhyan* means contemplation; *bhumisparsh* means invoking the earth to witness the attainment of Nirvana; and *dharmchakrapravartan* means turning the Wheel of Law.

The Buddha is often shown in yogic postures, with the *dharmchakra* or Wheel of Law sign prominent. On either side he is flanked by lions, with his hands held in the protective gesture. The expression remains one of radiant good nature.

The most impressive specimen from Mathura is a standing Buddha,

Facing page: Buddha's ground-touching posture—*bhumisparsha*—calls upon the earth to witness every good deed he has done and to protect him from the evil Mara's temptations. Sarnath Museum.

Following pages 90-91: The 'portraits' of different divinities, Bodhisattvas, Tantric masters and the historical Dalai Lamas in the Tibetan *tangkha* are recognizable through iconographic conventions. The legendary Guru Rimpoche Padmasambhava, believed to have exorcised Tibet of demons, is centrally placed in this *tangkha.*

88

seven feet tall. The superb haloes—*prabha mandala*—consist of concentric bands of great beauty with a multi-petal lotus radiating from the head. The Mathura figures seem to retain a strong echo of the Gandhara school and appear to be the products of an intermediate stage that came before Sarnath.

The specimens from Sarnath herald a total break as it were from the plastic creation of Mathura. These are suave executions of the artistic conception of the human body that came to dominate Indian sculpture. These Buddhas stand or are seated in slight detachment, exuding an aura of a being who has transcended the world of flux—*samsara*—and exists in a state of perfect awareness. This is the quality that permeates the entire image.

During the Gupta period (3rd to 5th century AD), the cave temples at Ajanta were constructed, with the walls adorned with breathtakingly beautiful frescoes that depict events from the Buddha's life. Ajanta has long been renowned as the stunning revelation of the Mahayana Buddhist vision. The paintings seem to uniquely complement the works of poets like Ashvagosh and philosophers like Nagarjuna. The subtle drawings pulsate with energy. Great concern for nature and tender humanism can be keenly felt. The realms of the senses and the intellect seem to fuse magically. There is gentle acceptance of transience—and death—which prepares the way to liberation.

The paintings at Ajanta serve a three-fold purpose—these decorate the walls, portray interesting and edifying characters and narrate a story with a moral. It is here at Ajanta that we encounter the Bodhisattva Avalokiteshvara Padmapani, in cave one, which shows, according to some, the very acme of Asian pictorial art. The Dying Princess in cave sixteen has received unalloyed praise from art critics and historians for its moving depiction of pathos and powerful story-telling.

Besides the Ajanta wall paintings, another, and a very different example of Buddhist painting is the Tibetan *tangkha*. The word 'tangkha' literally means a scroll and describes the physical object rather well. These are paintings on a piece of cloth that can be rolled up and stored when not on display. *Tangkhas* have been described very aptly as visual metaphors for spiritual encounters. Ranging from the fascinating to the grotesque they represent the splendid heritage of Tibetan art. The famous British explorer, Aurel Stein, discovered the oldest *tangkha* during an expedition to Tibet and this find now lies in the British Museum.

In the earliest *tangkhas*, the painters could not bear empty space and images were crammed with exuberant fancy, like the wild growth in a jungle. As for its purpose, initiates read into the *tangkhas* the

Facing page: The *tangkha* is much more than a painted scroll. It is considered an important aid to meditation. To experience mystic ecstasy, one is advised to 'enter' its consecrated space reverentially and follow the prescribed path.

Monks in deep meditation are a common sight in monasteries. Through meditation, a Buddhist eventually attains an assurance of the ineffable.

The gestures of the hands and fingers, known as *mudras*, described in Tantric Buddhism, are highly significant indicators of mental-emotional attitudes. Monks use the *dorje-vajra* (sceptre), the *ghanta* (bell) and the *mala* (rosary) to facilitate meditation. The Sanskrit word *mudra* means a seal. It is an integral part of the mind-voice-body trinity and accentuates or punctuates the ritual chant during worship. The dance-like choreography of the *mudra* during worship strives to raise the level of consciousness and align the psychic energy circuit.

The *dorje-vajra* (picture on far right, middle) is a symbol of absolute and irresistible power. It is compared to the diamond (*dorje* means master of stones in Tibetan). The *dorje* is in the sceptre shape with the centre representing a sphere— the gem of the universe—with potential forces indicated by spirals issuing from it. Holding the *dorje*, the adept seeks to focus all the conscious forces and psychic energies for meditational purposes. Coupled with the *dorje-vajra* is the *ghanta* (top, left) representing knowledge and symbolising the application of 'skillful means' to attain enlightenment. The rosary (bottom) usually contains 108 beads which are counted while the *mantras* are chanted.